Preface

Improving the security and safety of cyberspace—the interconnected information infrastructure of telecommunications networks and computer systems—has been an important priority of President Obama's Administration. Beginning with the *Cyberspace Policy Review: Assuring a Trusted and Resilient Information and Communications Infrastructure,*[1] the President mandated and launched a full spectrum of activities to eliminate or reduce cyberspace vulnerabilities and risks to the Nation's economic and social prosperity. In addition, the President challenged Federal agencies to develop a framework for game-changing cybersecurity research with the goal of fundamentally improving the security, safety, and trustworthiness of the Nation's digital infrastructure.

In December 2011 the National Science and Technology Council (NSTC) released *Trustworthy Cyberspace: Strategic Plan for the Federal Cybersecurity Research and Development Program,*[2] a framework for a set of coordinated Federal strategic priorities and objectives for cybersecurity research. The Strategic Plan was the result of a continuing dialogue between Federal agencies conducting cybersecurity research, agencies with cybersecurity as a critical facet of their mission, and leading industry and academic experts.

The 2011 Strategic Plan was the culmination of many efforts within the Federal Government, spearheaded by the Office of Science and Technology Policy (OSTP) and the Federal Networking and Information Technology Research and Development (NITRD) Program.[3] Three interagency forums coordinated the content of the report: the Cyber Security and Information Assurance Interagency Working Group (CSIA IWG), the Special Cyber Operations Research and Engineering (SCORE) IWG, and the Cyber Security and Information Assurance Research and Development Senior Steering Group (CSIA R&D SSG). Collectively, these groups represent efforts by the primary agencies conducting unclassified cybersecurity research within the Federal Government, including: the Defense Advanced Research Projects Agency (DARPA), Department of Energy (DOE), Department of Homeland Security (DHS), Intelligence Advanced Research Projects Activity (IARPA), National Institute of Standards and Technology (NIST), National Security Agency (NSA), National Science Foundation (NSF), Office of the Secretary of Defense (OSD), and Department of Defense Service research organizations in the Air Force, Army, and Navy.

Federal agencies have initiated and refined an ensemble of new and continuing prioritized research programs to address the challenges identified in the Strategic Plan. In addition to outlining agency strategies for addressing the goals of the Plan and summarizing key efforts directed at the principal research objectives, this report also presents potential areas in which further focus and support would be beneficial.

The four thrusts of the Strategic Plan and their corresponding areas of scientific research should not be taken as the whole of Federal activities in the area of cybersecurity. In fulfilling their mission goals, NITRD agencies have and will continue to engage in a diverse set of supplemental cybersecurity R&D activities on topics not directly addressed in the Strategic Plan or covered in this document. Many of these activities may be critical for the secure functioning of cyber systems of specific interest to agencies, but may not fall into the purview of the harmonized set of current priorities for the Federal cybersecurity R&D enterprise. Specifically, it is important to note that the unclassified research activities

---

[1] http://www.whitehouse.gov/assets/documents/Cyberspace_Policy_Review_final.pdf
[2] http://www.whitehouse.gov/sites/default/files/microsites/ostp/fed_cybersecurity_rd_strategic_plan_2011.pdf
[3] http://www.nitrd.gov

outlined are only one portion of the work of the Federal cybersecurity R&D enterprise, of which classified activities are an important additional component.

In February 2013, the President issued Executive Order 13636 (EO 13636), "Improving Critical Infrastructure Cybersecurity,"[4] and Presidential Policy Directive 21 (PPD-21), "Critical Infrastructure Security and Resilience."[5] Executive Order 13636 states "the cyber threat to critical infrastructure continues to grow and represents one of the most serious national security challenges we must confront. The national and economic security of the United States depends on the reliable functioning of the Nation's critical infrastructure in the face of such threats. It is the policy of the United States to enhance the security and resilience of the Nation's critical infrastructure and to maintain a cyber-environment that encourages efficiency, innovation, and economic prosperity while promoting safety, security, business confidentiality, privacy, and civil liberties."

Within these two documents, the President has specified a new roadmap of activities and goals that the Federal Government must undertake to ensure the cybersecurity of the Nation's critical infrastructure, outlining a plan of policy coordination, information sharing, privacy and civil liberties protection, and the development of frameworks to identify and address cybersecurity risks. Presidential Policy Directive 21 explicitly outlines the roles and responsibilities for different agencies within this directive, including for cybersecurity R&D, specifically:

1. Promoting R&D to enable the secure and resilient design and construction of critical infrastructure and accompanying cyber technology;

2. Enhancing modeling capabilities for determining potential impacts of incident or threat scenarios on critical infrastructure, as well as cascading effects on other sectors;

3. Facilitating initiatives to incentivize cybersecurity investments and the adoption of critical infrastructure design features that strengthen all-hazards security and resilience; and

4. Prioritizing efforts to support the strategic guidance issued by the Secretary of Homeland Security.

The first three goals in PPD-21 are already areas of focus within the Strategic Plan, or outlined as a prospective future priority area within this report. The last goal will require renewed interagency dialogue and coordination to synchronize the Secretary of Homeland Security's efforts with the extensive and ongoing Federal cybersecurity R&D enterprise outlined in this document.

As the NITRD CSIA IWG co-chairs, we are gratified by the exceptional level of cybersecurity research coordination that the Strategic Plan has initiated, and we are confident that a continuing focus on the objectives of this Plan and its coordination by NITRD groups will contribute significantly to securing cyberspace.

Douglas Maughan, DHS S&T
William Newhouse, NIST

Co-Chairs
NITRD Cyber Security and Information Assurance Interagency Working Group (CSIA IWG)

---

[4] http://www.gpo.gov/fdsys/pkg/FR-2013-02-19/pdf/2013-03915.pdf
[5] http://www.whitehouse.gov/the-press-office/2013/02/12/presidential-policy-directive-critical-infrastructure-security-and-resil

Implementing the Federal Cybersecurity R&D Strategy

1 Introduction

The Nation's security, economic progress, and modern lifestyle are increasingly dependent on cyberinfrastructure—the vast, interconnected information networks, communications technologies, and computer systems that handle the processing and flow of information across the many distributed environments and resources of cyberspace. This increasing reliance must be matched with assurances that information and communication technologies can securely support the core activities underpinning cyberspace. However, the history of the creation of the Internet has left a legacy in its structure and design that makes securing cyberinfrastructure today a massive technical challenge. The Internet was originally developed to support a new mode of communication and information sharing between scientists at different institutions. Since all the users were members of a relatively small and exclusive group, flexibility and scalability, not security, were the key attributes of its design. While these attributes have enabled the innovations that have driven rapid growth and adoption of the technology, the community of Internet users is no longer a small and friendly club, but rather a global ecosystem of interconnected players with diverse needs, capabilities, and motives. It is very difficult now to retrofit trust mechanisms into the Internet and to achieve the level of security required for cyberinfrastructure and the systems dependent on it.

In December 2011 the NSTC released *Trustworthy Cyberspace: Strategic Plan for the Federal Cybersecurity Research and Development Program*, outlining a vision for the research needed to develop game-changing technologies to neutralize attacks on the cyber systems of today, and to establish scientific foundations to meet the challenges of securing the cyber systems of tomorrow. The Strategic Plan surfaced intersections of common interest and mutual benefit in cybersecurity research; outlined specific research and development areas that span multiple disciplines; and emphasized collaboration among researchers and technical experts in government, industry, academia, and international contexts.

Since the release of the Strategic Plan, Federal agencies have responded vigorously by adapting their existing cybersecurity R&D programs and initiating new activities that align with the Plan's strategic priorities. This report summarizes the broad Federal response, highlighting the specific research activities that agencies are supporting. This report finds that, since the release of the Strategic Plan, agencies have coordinated successfully to minimize duplication among R&D efforts and made excellent progress in creating and leveraging partnerships with other agencies and external parties on key research areas. Agencies have also put proper focus on transitioning research to practice and maximizing the impact of their R&D investments.

Looking forward to the near future, the framework outlined in the Strategic Plan remains pertinent and viable; the four strategic thrusts of **Inducing Change**, **Developing Scientific Foundations**, **Maximizing Impact**, and **Accelerating Transition to Practice** are still the key areas of Federal action needed to help create a cyber-safe Nation. However, given recent advancements in technology, new needs, and an improved understanding of the foundations of cybersecurity, additional areas within each thrust have emerged that require emphasis. Some of these areas of emphasis are discussed in this document. In addition, two broader areas for cybersecurity research have emerged as critical to the function of our Nation and to the fulfillment of agency mission goals: **Privacy and Protected Disclosure** and the

Security of Cyber-Physical Systems. Though both can be considered facets of the research themes within the 2011 Strategic Plan, they have risen in importance and warrant explicit highlighting as priority research areas.

As the emergence of new technologies and capabilities drives increasing dependency on cyberinfrastructure, the Federal Government must match the growth in information and communication technology with an expanded investment in cybersecurity R&D. Research into the newly identified priority research areas outlined in this document must be conducted in tandem with ongoing activities. Reflecting this need for more investment, the President's FY 2015 budget request proposes $715 million for unclassified cybersecurity R&D activities through the NITRD agencies – an increase of $62 million over the $653 million in actual expenditures for FY 2013.[6]

2 Overview and Scope

This report on the implementation of the Federal cybersecurity R&D strategy follows the basic outline of the 2011 Strategic Plan, organizing topical areas into four strategic thrusts and, within each thrust, into key research themes and focus areas. The report covers two main areas: a summary of R&D activities at each of the primary NITRD agencies (Sections 4-5) and an analysis of the Federal response and proposals for next steps (Sections 6-7). Section 3 restates the framework of four strategic thrusts articulated in the Plan, establishing the context for the subsequent sections. Section 4 provides an overview of agency responses to the Strategic Plan and identifies the relationship of the responses to the four strategic thrusts. Section 5 gives an overview of the types of activities pursued within each of the thrusts and highlights specific examples of relevant programs and projects. Section 6 analyzes the accomplishments, gaps, and overlaps in the Federal response to the 2011 Plan, and identifies emerging areas where additional emphasis may be warranted. Section 7 outlines next steps to be taken by NITRD in continuing the dialogue, both within the Federal Government and externally, to address the Strategic Plan.

As part of this review, public comments[7] on the Strategic Plan were solicited to gain insights from experts in industry, academia, and the public. These comments enhance understanding of the research and implementation challenges of the Strategic Plan, and continue the open dialogue that is needed between the government and the technical community at-large to help refine and improve the Plan. Key comments and responses are noted within the pertinent sections of this document, as applicable.

In addition to discussing the topics presented in the Strategic Plan, the public comments stressed the importance of policy, education, usability, funding, transparency, and accountability as critical aspects of a responsive national cybersecurity enterprise. Although these topics are outside the scope of an R&D-focused Strategic Plan, it is worth noting that many agencies have programs that target some of these areas; for example, NSF is funding two research centers around the social, behavioral, and economic perspectives of cybersecurity.[8] Within this broader social and technological context for cybersecurity, the NITRD Program identified "Cyber Economic Incentives" as a high-impact priority and explicitly targeted research in this area. In the future, as other topics move toward the forefront and become key enablers or barriers to maintaining a secure cyberspace, NITRD agencies and the Administration are prepared to respond with additional R&D focused on those topics.

---

[6] http://www.nitrd.gov/pubs/2015supplement/FY2015NITRDSupplement.pdf

[7] Submitted comments are available in their entirety at:
http://www.nitrd.gov/fileupload/files/RFC_Submissions_Fed_Cybersecurity_RD_Strat_Plan_20130114.pdf

[8] One center at Harvard University focuses on privacy issues in social science research, while the other, which is a collaboration among George Washington University, the University of California at San Diego, and the International Computer Science Institute, aims to develop an empirical basis for social-economic perspectives.

Finally, it is important to note that this document outlines only the research activities conducted by the Federal Government in the unclassified domain. Scoping of unclassified research priorities is part of a greater research context that includes U.S. Government-funded classified R&D activities, ongoing domestic private sector research, and international cybersecurity research and development activities.

3 Summary of the Federal Cybersecurity R&D Strategy

The Strategic Plan provides a framework of four strategic thrusts to organize activities and drive progress in cybersecurity R&D:

- **Inducing Change** – Utilizing game-changing themes to direct efforts towards understanding the underlying root causes of known current threats with the goal of disrupting the status quo with radically different approaches to improve the security of the critical cyber systems and infrastructure that serve society.

- **Developing Scientific Foundations** – Developing an organized, cohesive scientific foundation to the body of knowledge that informs the field of cybersecurity through adoption of a systematic, rigorous, and disciplined scientific approach. Promoting the discovery of laws, hypothesis testing, repeatable experimental designs, standardized data-gathering methods, metrics, common terminology, and critical analysis that engenders reproducible results and rationally based conclusions.

- **Maximizing Research Impact** – Catalyzing integration across the game-changing R&D themes, cooperation between governmental and private-sector communities, collaboration across international borders, and strengthening linkages to other national priorities, such as health IT and Smart Grid.

- **Accelerating Transition to Practice** – Focusing efforts to ensure adoption and implementation of the powerful new technologies and strategies that emerge from the research themes, and the activities to build a scientific foundation so as to create measurable improvements in the cybersecurity landscape.

4 Agency Missions Aligned with the Federal Cybersecurity R&D Strategy

The Strategic Plan identifies high priority cyber capabilities that hold promise for enabling fundamental improvements in the security and trustworthiness of cyberspace. To achieve these capabilities, the Plan defines an R&D framework that organizes objectives and activities across a range of R&D efforts, including those that require coordination across multiple agencies and those that an individual agency might support in the context of its particular mission, capabilities, and expertise. For example, NSF, which serves to promote the progress of science, contributes to the Plan's objectives by funding academic research on the scientific foundations of security. DARPA, which aims to maintain the technological superiority of the U.S. military, contributes to the Plan's objectives by sponsoring the development of revolutionary, high-payoff defense technologies to maximize research impact.

Collectively, the agencies execute a coordinated portfolio of R&D activities from basic science to mission-specific capabilities. No single agency addresses all the priority areas in the Strategic Plan nor should it. Instead, it is the many different agency efforts comprising the Federal cybersecurity R&D enterprise that, with guidance from the Strategic Plan and coordination through NITRD, enables progress towards the Plan's goals. This section summarizes the unique aspects of agency research strategies for addressing the goals and challenges outlined in the Strategic Plan.

Air Force Research Laboratory (AFRL)

AFRL's efforts in cybersecurity aim to create a firm, trustable foundation in cyberspace, and then to build assured mission capabilities upon it. New technologies are needed to be aware of missions and threats, compute optimal assurance solutions, and implement protection as needed via mission agility or infrastructure reinforcement. The capabilities developed through this research will be more agile and resilient than current solutions, providing the ability to avoid, fight through, survive, and recover from advanced cyber threats. They will also be more effective at engaging and optimizing the role of humans in cyberspace operations.

Army Research Laboratory (ARL)

ARL's mission is to provide the science, technology, and analysis that underpin full-spectrum military operations. Within its mission, ARL contributes to a number of the Strategic Plan's objectives with a particular focus on Moving Target technologies within its **Cyber Maneuver Initiative**. The Cyber Maneuver Initiative aims to improve defense against advanced persistent threats by creating dynamic attack surfaces for protected systems, and includes research in dynamic operating system maneuverability, application diversity, network agility, cyber deception, predictive cyber threat modeling, and cognitive reasoning and feedback to maximize maneuver effectiveness in tactical environments.

Defense Advanced Research Projects Agency (DARPA)

DARPA is the principal agency within the Department of Defense for high-risk, high-payoff research, development, and demonstration of new technologies and systems that serve the warfighter and the Nation's defense. DARPA's R&D efforts in cybersecurity strongly support the Moving Target and Tailored Trustworthy Spaces themes. In particular, DARPA's **Information Assurance and Survivability Program** seeks to draw on biological and immune systems as inspiration for radically re-thinking computer hardware, software, and system designs. Such systems will be able to detect, diagnose, and respond to attacks by employing their own innate and adaptive immune systems. Furthermore, in response to attacks, such systems will also be capable of dynamically adapting and improving their defensive capabilities over time. As in biological systems, the cyber systems will dynamically diversify, increasing their resiliency and survivability, and that of their individual, constituent computers.

Department of Energy (DOE)

A key mission of the DOE Office of Electricity Delivery and Energy Reliability (OE) is to enhance the reliability and resiliency of the Nation's energy infrastructure. Within DOE OE's **Cybersecurity for Energy Delivery Systems (CEDS) Program**, cybersecurity R&D is tailored to the unique performance requirements, designs, and operational environments of energy delivery systems. The CEDS Program operates with the goal that, by 2020, resilient energy delivery systems are designed, installed, operated, and maintained to survive cyber-incidents while sustaining critical functions. To help achieve this vision, OE fosters and actively engages in collaborations among all energy stakeholders – utility, vendor, national lab, and academic. Through these collaborations, OE seeks to solve hand-in-hand with industry the "right problems," and to transition next-generation research from the national labs and academia into commercial products operating in the energy sector. The Strategic Plan research themes, particularly Designed-In Security and Tailored Trustworthy Spaces are strongly supported by the strategies and milestones outlined in the CEDS Program.

Other elements of DOE also perform related cybersecurity research. The Advanced Scientific Computing Research (ASCR) Program, which is part of the Office of Science, sponsors research to support DOE's world leadership in scientific computation. Security of networks and middleware is a critical element in the ASCR Next Generation Networking research program. The National Nuclear Security Administration (NNSA) within DOE also sponsors cybersecurity research to support its unique mission requirements.

Department of Homeland Security (DHS)

The DHS Science and Technology Directorate Cyber Security Division (DHS S&T CSD) focuses on applied research and development, test, evaluation, and transition for technologies to support civilian Federal, state, and local governments and private sector unclassified needs to protect the Nation's cyber infrastructure. Of particular interest to DHS are technologies that can be developed and transitioned to commercial products or used in Federal, state, and local government systems. DHS S&T CSD has promoted innovation and accelerated transition to practice by using Broad Agency Announcements (BAA) to solicit research proposals, supporting the **Small Business Innovation Research (SBIR)** program, participating in and initiating public-private partnerships, and collaborating with Federal agencies and international partners through joint project funding and management. In FY 2011, DHS S&T CSD issued BAA 11-02 which solicited proposals for R&D in 14 technical areas, spanning all research themes of the Strategic Plan.

Intelligence Advanced Research Projects Activity (IARPA)

IARPA's cybersecurity research is spearheaded by its Office of Safe and Secure Operations (SSO), which aims to counter emerging adversary potential to ensure the U.S. Intelligence Community's operational effectiveness in a globally interdependent and networked environment. SSO's research portfolio is organized into three areas: computational power, trustworthy components, and safe and secure systems. Objectives within the computational power area include developing revolutionary advances in science and engineering to solve problems intractable with today's computers, focusing on the fundamental elements of quantum computing systems, and exploring the feasibility of a superconducting computer. In the trustworthy components area, research programs focus on understanding and manipulating very small-scale electronics, obtaining mission-worthy chips from state-of-the-art, but untrusted fabrication facilities, and gaining functionality from un-pedigreed software without placing mission systems at risk. Finally, research in the safe and secure systems area has a broad objective of safeguarding the integrity of missions in a hostile environment. Some of the current projects focus on enabling collaboration without wholesale sharing of data through privacy-preserving search techniques. Research in both the trustworthy components and safe and secure systems areas contributes directly to the Tailored Trustworthy Spaces research theme.

National Institute of Standards and Technology (NIST)

NIST's Information Technology Laboratory (ITL) is a recognized thought leader in cryptography, identity management, key management, mobile security, risk management, security automation, security of networked systems, foundations of measurement science for information systems, secure virtualization, cloud security, trusted roots of hardware, usability and security, and vulnerability management. ITL is comprised of six divisions; each has ongoing work that moves the Nation towards the end-state vision of the Cybersecurity R&D Strategic Plan. In particular, the NIST Software and Systems Division (SSD) works with industry, academia, and other government agencies to increase trust and confidence in deployed software, standards and testing tools for today's software infrastructures and tomorrow's next-generation software systems, and conformance testing. Additionally, the NIST Computer Security Division (CSD) within ITL leads the Government's efforts in risk management, identity management, key management, security automation, mobile security, trusted roots for hardware, vulnerability management, and cryptography. CSD's activities in key management, multi-factor authentication, and identity management strongly contribute to the Tailored Trustworthy Spaces theme. Among its recent priorities, CSD's efforts in information security continuous monitoring support the Moving Target theme—by developing tools and specifications that maintain ongoing awareness of information security, vulnerabilities, and threats to support organizational risk management decisions. The NIST National Cybersecurity Center of Excellence (NCCoE) and National Strategy for Trusted Identities in Cyberspace (NSTIC) Program Management Office are focused on driving adoption of cybersecurity and identity management standards and best practices to support measurable improvements in the cybersecurity landscape.

National Security Agency (NSA)

NSA has several research efforts exploring the Tailored Trustworthy Spaces theme, including exploration of risk through behavioral analytics and large-scale data analysis, novel means to detect modifications to computing systems and network analytics, and efforts to customize system controls. NSA is also exploring Moving Target technologies. By conducting a full scope analysis of the Moving Target problem and solution space, NSA plans to develop "movement" prototypes and evaluate several critical enabling functions. In partnership with the DoD, the agency produced a survey of current Moving Target techniques, thereby enabling a cost-benefit analysis that will take into account different approaches and technologies, the potential impact Moving Target protections may have on mission operations, the costs and overheads associated with implementation, and the overall effectiveness of the movement response. Additionally, NSA is supporting activities that foster an interdisciplinary collaborative community around the science of security, including a virtual organization and four university-based multidisciplinary research centers.

National Science Foundation (NSF)

NSF invests in cybersecurity research through several programs, including the Directorate of Engineering (ENG) programs in Communications, Circuits, and Sensing-Systems (CCSS) and Energy, Power, and Adaptive Systems (EPAS). A major program in cybersecurity is spearheaded by the NSF Directorate of Computer and Information Science and Engineering (CISE), in collaboration with the Directorates of Education and Human Resources (EHR), Engineering (ENG), Mathematical and Physical Sciences (MPS), and Social, Behavioral & Economic Sciences (SBE). NSF's solicitation for the **Secure and Trustworthy Cyberspace (SaTC) Program** provides funding to university investigators for research activities on all four Strategic Plan thrusts, with an explicit option for transition to practice projects. The solicitation provides funding for projects related to cybersecurity education, as well as social, behavioral, and economic perspectives on cybersecurity. Another major program is **CyberCorps: Scholarship for Service (SFS)** led by the EHR Directorate. This program supports cybersecurity education and workforce development. NSF's program is distinguished from other agency efforts by its comprehensive nature, and by the strong role of research on cybersecurity foundations.

Office of Naval Research (ONR)

ONR cybersecurity strategies focus on long- and medium-term scientific and technology areas that have the potential for delivering significant improvements in the robustness, resiliency, security, and operational effectiveness of cyber environments. ONR's cybersecurity research contributes strongly to the objectives identified in the Moving Target, Tailored Trustworthy Spaces, and Designed-In Security areas. The Moving Target theme is particularly supported by the **Robust and Autonomic Computing Systems Program**, a long-term initiative for exploring architectures and approaches for future adaptive computing systems. Research in the Tailored Trustworthy Spaces area is supported by the **Fabric Project** a medium-term project providing strong, principled security guarantees based on explicitly stated security policies, and does so for distributed systems with complex, incomplete, and changing trust between participants. Additional programs such as **Automation in Cryptology, Software Efficiency Reclamation, Computer Network Defense and Information Assurance,** and **Quantum Information Sciences** contribute to the Strategic Plan by developing novel capabilities and technologies across the research themes. At the Georgia Institute of Technology, ONR-funded researchers investigated the theory and models for botnets, and developed state of the art algorithms, methods, and tools for detecting and tracking botnets and their command and control. Their research has been invaluable for the DoD, as well as the tools developed and now in use by the FBI for taking down botnets and tracking down bot-masters and individual operators. Additionally, ONR promotes underexplored research topics that have promising impacts on cybersecurity. For example, at the University of California, ONR is supporting a technical investigation of the underground economy that allows botnets to exist.

Office of the Secretary of Defense (OSD)
DoD's cybersecurity science and technology programs emphasize game-changing research over incremental approaches, and enhance the organizational ties and experimental infrastructure needed to accelerate transition of new technologies into practice. To strengthen its ability to pursue a coordinated set of objectives and a shared vision in cybersecurity, the Assistant Secretary of Defense for Research and Engineering (ASD(R&E)) formed the **DoD Cyber S&T Community of Interest (DoD Cyber COI)**. The DoD has specialized needs in cybersecurity due to the nature of its national security and warfighting mission. The DoD Cyber COI was charged with developing a DoD Cyber S&T problem statement, challenge areas that address warfighter requirements, a research framework, priority technology areas, and, in particular, a Cyber S&T Roadmap of current and needed research in cybersecurity.

The Cyber S&T Roadmap lays out four areas of research: Foundations of Trust, Resilient Infrastructure, Agile Operations, and Assuring Effective Missions. All four areas relate strongly to the Designed-In Security theme, strengthening different attributes of security through development, design, and validation methods, component and system design, algorithms, protocols, and architecture. The Foundations of Trust area contributes particularly to the Tailored Trustworthy Spaces theme. The Resilient Infrastructure and Agile Operations areas support the Moving Target theme. All four Roadmap areas have research challenges that will contribute to the foundational Science of Security.

5 Implementing the Strategic Plan: Agency Highlights and Accomplishments

5.1 Inducing Change

Achieving enduring trustworthiness of cyberspace requires new paradigms that re-balance the security asymmetries of today's cyber environment. The major challenges and new paradigms needed to overcome them motivate R&D agendas in four research themes:

- **Moving Target**: The cost of attacks is asymmetric, favoring the attacker, and so defenders must increase the cost of attack and employ methods that enable them to continue to operate in the face of attack;

- **Tailored Trustworthy Spaces**: The burden of simultaneously satisfying all the requirements of an ideal cybersecurity solution is impossibly high, and so we must enable sub-spaces in cyberspace to support different security policies and different security services for different types of interactions;

- **Designed-In Security**: The prevalent software design and development methodologies and tools handicap designers' capability to design, develop, and evolve high-assurance systems that are resistant to attacks, and so we must increase our ability to utilize assurance-focused engineering practices that enable reasoning about a diversity of quality attributes (security, safety, reliability, etc.) while providing the evidence necessary to prove the system's resistance to vulnerabilities;

- **Cyber Economic Incentives**: The lack of meaningful metrics and economically sound decision making in security misallocates resources, and so we must promote economic principles in identifying and realigning economic and social incentives that encourage the broad use of good cybersecurity practices and deter illicit activities.

The four research themes provide a shared and unifying set of objectives with the most promising impacts on national cybersecurity issues. Federal cybersecurity research strategies focus on the research themes and on enabling component technologies supportive of, or required by, these themes. However, the themes do not preclude agencies from undertaking other research activities that are necessary to fulfilling their missions. Overlying these challenges is the need for agencies to achieve impactful results in their mission responsibilities balanced with operational costs, scalability, and usability. These additional attributes are critical in enabling the smooth transition to practice of cybersecurity research, which is discussed in further detail in Section 5.4.

5.1.1 Moving Target

The vision and goals of the Moving Target research theme are as follows:

Vision
Develop, evaluate, and deploy diverse mechanisms and strategies that dynamically shift and change over time in order to increase complexity and costs for attackers, limit the exposure of vulnerabilities and opportunities for attack, and increase system resiliency.

Goals
- Design resilient systems that operate reliably in compromised environments
- Increase the cost of staging and executing attacks
- Shift from reactive security postures to active preemptive postures
- Develop Moving Target mechanisms that create disruptions for the adversaries, but not for legitimate users
- Develop the ability to optimize Moving Target mechanisms against various attacks and disruptions

At a high level, the research supported by agencies within the Moving Target theme can be grouped along several contributing characteristics:

- Frameworks
- Techniques
- Scientific foundations

5.1.1.1 Frameworks
A number of research activities include investigating and developing novel frameworks for managing systems that employ Moving Target mechanisms and strategies. For example, DHS, NSF, and DARPA are funding research efforts that use biological concepts—such as those related to immune systems, genetic algorithms, and social insect behaviors—to create distributed cyber systems that are flexible when responding to a cyber-attack. In the same way that biological systems are constantly aware, adapting, and evolving, these systems are designed to detect new anomalous code or attack methods, adapt and

repair after a cyber-attack, and cope with new vulnerabilities that can be introduced over time. These "nature-inspired solutions" were called out as a focus area in the Moving Target theme of the Strategic Plan, and many agencies have coalesced around the concept in novel and unique ways.

Spotlight on DARPA –

Clean-Slate Design of Resilient, Adaptive, Secure Hosts (CRASH) and Mission-oriented Resilient Clouds (MRC) Programs

Announced in June 2010, DARPA's **Clean-Slate Design of Resilient, Adaptive, Secure Hosts (CRASH) Program** is focused on designing new and revolutionary architectures that make computer systems highly resistant to cyber-attacks. The objective is to design systems that are able to adapt and continue rendering useful services after a successful attack, learn from previous attacks on how to guard against and cope with future attacks, and repair themselves after attacks have succeeded.

CRASH has initiated projects in three biologically inspired areas: The *Innate Immunity* area has the goal of eliminating all common technical vulnerabilities, with solutions focused primarily on hardware, operating systems, middleware, and formal methods. The *Adaptive Immunity* area works in cooperation with *Innate* components at a higher level in the stack and includes projects to develop techniques for identifying, diagnosing, and recovering from new attacks. The *Dynamic Diversity* area is inspired by the biological concept of diversity leading to survivability. In this area, techniques are being developed that make each computer different from every other computer, and make each computer differ from itself over time. This raises an attacker's work factor while maintaining system manageability.

One of CRASH's achievements is the Diversity Compiler: compiler technologies that make it possible to create diverse versions of applications and operating systems that behave in exactly the same way under normal use, but do not share vulnerabilities among them. By changing characteristics, such as the specific machine instructions a program uses or the way it is placed into memory, users see no changes in program behavior; attackers, however, are forced to break into each unique instance and are prevented from reusing a single attack across millions of computers. The CRASH Program has also developed a prototype hardware-software system to enforce a number of formal assurance and protection principles. For example, it can restrict access within a host to only what is essential for a given program, following the principle of least privilege.

Building on the successes of CRASH, DARPA's **Mission-oriented Resilient Clouds (MRC) Program** is developing technologies to detect, diagnose, and respond to attacks in cloud computing systems so that cloud applications and infrastructure can continue functioning while under attack. These technologies use cloud resources to relocate computations so that attackers are not able to find them, and to induce artificial diversity across hosts so that no two hosts present the same configuration to the attacker. Additionally, resources can be grouped to provide collective defense, automatically detect and diagnose any system penetration, automatically develop work-arounds and patches, and distribute these solutions around the cloud so that the entire system learns from each individual host. Ultimately, the system as a whole becomes more secure and resilient than any individual host.

Spotlight on ONR –

Robust Autonomic Host Program

ONR's **Robust Autonomic Host Program** is focused on developing computing systems that can self-heal, operate under attack with reduced capabilities, employ artificial diversity to increase resilience, and engage in disinformation as an element of Moving Target defense. Initiated in FY 2011, this program supports exploratory and experimental research towards achieving robust, resilient, and autonomic computing in the future. The program covers wide areas of research and engineering applicable to computing infrastructure, including efficient and adaptive data-acquisition and monitoring, machine intelligence, machine reasoning and strategic planning, automated diagnostics, artificial diversity, and automated strategic deception. An autonomic computing system that continuously assesses its own state, health, capabilities and limitations, and adapts to the situation at cyber speed, can maximize mission success while reducing operational cost.

5.1.1.2 Techniques

A significant portion of Moving Target research involves developing techniques that modify system characteristics in one or more dimensions. For example:

- Policies – risk adaptive policies, movement scheduling

- System of systems – non-persistent virtual machines, system self-cleansing, machine rotations

- Data – secure distributed data chunking and decentralization, data encryption

- Networks – dynamic networking, dynamic Domain Name System (DNS), Internet Protocol (IP) address randomization

- Software – source code diversity, just-in-time compiling, disposable applications

- System – diversity in operating systems, instruction set randomization

- Hardware – multicore processing, cache randomization

At Sandia National Laboratories, both AFRL and DOE have programs to develop technologies that can rapidly change or randomize network addresses and device paths; from an attacker's perspective, this results in a constantly changing and difficult to understand network layout. IARPA is conducting research in software techniques to automate processes for modifying software code to neutralize vulnerabilities. DHS's Moving Target Defense Program focuses on a wide variety of Moving Target techniques within different layers of the hardware and software stack.

Spotlight on AFRL –

Cyber Agility Initiative

AFRL has been at the forefront of Moving Target research with initiatives such as the **Cyber Agility Initiative**, announced in FY 2011. This initiative's objective is to make it harder for a determined adversary to succeed by increasing agility, diversity, and redundancy, and by disrupting attack plans and execution.

In FY 2012 AFRL launched the **Polymorphic Machines and Enclaves Program** within the Cyber Agility Initiative. Polymorphic machines use continuously changing computer and system characteristics in a manner that is controlled by the transformation and diversification process, and yet appear to an attacker to be a randomly shifting target space. At the same time, however, the systems maintain transparency and utility for authorized users. The concept of polymorphic machines is extended to the entire network in the Polymorphic Enclaves Program, which aims to create rapidly shifting network architectures with automated agility and diversity mechanisms to modify or morph the network continually, dynamically, and unpredictably into secure operational modes, both before and during attacks.

In addition to these new programs, the Cyber Agility Initiative is responsible for the successful **Active Repositioning in Cyberspace for Synchronized Evasion (ARCSYNE)** technology, which is entering into pilot projects with other agencies. This technology employs IP address hopping to create an agile and stealthy network where the network identity of hosts changes rapidly to confuse attackers. In a one-year follow-up project, started in Q4 of 2012, DHS is funding expansion of the technology to include higher network speeds and network management capabilities. The expected outcome at the end of this project will be a fully functioning network appliance unit that can operate as close to 10 Gbps as possible and change IP addresses in the network at least 10 times/second.

Spotlight on IARPA –

Securely Taking On New Executable Software Of Uncertain Provenance (STONESOUP) Program

The IARPA **Securely Taking On New Executable Software Of Uncertain Provenance (STONESOUP) Program** seeks to automate the detection and mitigation of security vulnerabilities in software applications while diversifying program code, so that residual vulnerabilities are harder to exploit. STONESOUP is also investigating novel techniques for randomizing, rewriting, or monitoring software application code so that an adversary will not be able to predict the location of instructions or data needed to launch malicious exploits. The goal of the program is to be able to mitigate security vulnerabilities of software with uncertain provenance automatically without relying on expensive and limited manual security evaluations.

The program began in September 2010 and is slated to end in November 2014. Phase 2 currently has four funded projects developing techniques for sound analysis of software, for automatically inferring reasonable security policies, and for automatically mitigating vulnerabilities without expert human interaction. Phase 1 was successfully completed, demonstrating the ability to neutralize (render unexploitable) over 75% of two types of seeded vulnerabilities in 10,000 line programs while preserving normal program behaviors. Phase 2 goals are to increase the size of programs to 100,000 lines of code, to increase the number of vulnerability types to four, and to demonstrate that 80% of vulnerabilities are automatically mitigated. Future Phase 3 goals include 500,000 line programs, six types of vulnerabilities, and requirements for a 90% rate of vulnerability neutralization with no more than a 10% increase in runtime overhead.

Spotlight on DHS –

Moving Target Defense Program

DHS's **Moving Target Defense Program** pursues new capabilities and technologies in several Moving Target areas. These include (1) integration of self-cleaning, intrusion-tolerant servers with reactive systems, (2) active kernel updates that keep system attack surfaces dynamic, (3) IP version 6 (IPv6) integration with IP-address hopping technology, (4) development of obfuscation and virtual instance randomization technologies, (5) binary program randomization, (6) translation of insect colony behavioral models into algorithms for rapidly detecting malware, and (7) applying bio-sequence analysis to discover anomalous sequences of transactions within networks.

The program was initiated under a 2012 DHS BAA which awarded four contracts and five SBIR awards. Current work includes innovative hardware cache designs to increase resiliency, improvements to the ARCSYNE system, novel bio-inspired approaches to intrusion and anomalous behavior detection, a multi-kernel OS architecture that increases system resilience and minimizes the effect of Moving Target Defense on mission-critical tasks, IP-hopping utilizing IPv6, and Multi-layer Ever-changing Self-defense Services (MESS) that are both resilient and manageable. The bio-inspired solutions may ultimately change the current approach used for developing intrusion detection systems. New attack methods will quickly be detected rather than relying on the knowledge of existing, known malicious software or cyber-attacks.

5.1.1.3 Scientific Foundations of Moving Target

Integral to Moving Target research is a scientific foundation for understanding and analyzing the effectiveness of Moving Target frameworks and mechanisms. These analyses show what classes of attacks are stopped by particular mechanisms, how to compare different approaches, and how to assess the effectiveness of the techniques.

Scientific foundations of Moving Target are the focus of the Army Research Office's (ARO) Moving Target Defense Program, a five-year, multidisciplinary university research project that began in July 2013. The goal of the program is to establish scientific foundations of adaptive systems that are robust, resilient, and survivable against cyber-attacks. In conjunction with the ARO effort, and also beginning in late FY 2013, ARL has established a new collaborative venture—the **Cyber Security Collaborative Research Alliance (CRA)**—that seeks to advance interdisciplinary, theoretical foundations of cyber science in the context of Army networks. NSA is also contributing to the scientific foundations of Moving Target by developing an assessment and taxonomies of techniques and methodologies for their analysis, and by having organized the first National Symposium on Moving Target Research, held in Annapolis, MD in June 2012.[9]

---

[9] http://cps-vo.org/group/mtrs

Spotlight on ARL –

Cyber Security Collaborative Research Alliance (CRA)

ARL has established a new collaborative venture—the **Cyber Security Collaborative Research Alliance**—that seeks to advance the inter-disciplinary, theoretical foundations of cyber science in the context of Army networks, focused in part on cyber agility in its inter-relations with theories of cyber detection of malicious activities, characterization of risks, and cross-cutting issues of psychosocial aspects in cyber agility. The CRA consists of academia, industry, and government researchers working jointly to solve complex problems. The *Agility Research Area* seeks to develop theories and models to support planning and control of cyber maneuver (i.e., "maneuver" in the space of network characteristics and topologies) that would describe how control and end-state of the maneuver are influenced by fundamental properties of threats, such as might be rapidly inferred from limited observations of a new, recently observed threat. The *Risk Research Area* seeks to develop theories and models that relate fundamental properties and features of dynamic risk assessment algorithms to the fundamental properties of dynamic cyber threats, Army's networks, and defensive mechanisms. The *Detection Research Area* seeks to develop theories and models that relate properties and capabilities of cyber threat detection and recognition processes/mechanisms to properties of a malicious activity, and of properties of Army networks. This research should inform development of approaches to rapid adaptation (potentially in the midst of a battle) of a detection technique or algorithm as new threats emerge. Psychosocial effects will be studied across all three areas; since teams of human defenders will likely be the key link in cyber defense, a theoretical understanding of the socio-cognitive factors that impact the decision making of the user/soldier, defender/analyst, and adversary needs to be developed.

5.1.2 Tailored Trustworthy Spaces

The vision and goals of the Tailored Trustworthy Spaces research theme are as follows:

Vision
- Create flexible and distributed trust environments that can support a range of functional and policy requirements arising from a wide spectrum of activities in cyberspace.
- Support operating capabilities across multiple dimensions, including confidentiality, anonymity, data and system integrity, provenance, availability, and performance.

Goals
- Enable trustworthy computing in untrustworthy environments
- Develop a common framework that supports varying trustworthy space policies and context-specific trust services for different types of actions and transactions
- Develop rules, measurable metrics of trustworthiness, flexible trust negotiation tools, configuration decision support capabilities, and the ability to perform informed trust analysis

Research in Tailored Trustworthy Spaces can be organized along the following high-level dimensions:

- Characterization
- Trust negotiation
- Operations
- Privacy

5.1.2.1 Characterization

Research in the characterization of Tailored Trustworthy Spaces aims to identify and specify elements that describe the space, translate operational requirements into policies, define tailoring requirements, and translate tailoring requirements into executable rules.

Agency research efforts also support the characterization of specific application areas of Tailored Trustworthy Spaces. For example, NSF is funding researchers at Carnegie Mellon University to investigate the semantics and enforcement of privacy policies, particularly for healthcare. Legal requirements for healthcare records are different from those associated with traditional computer security access in that first, they often include restrictions on future uses of data in addition to current uses, and second, these policies can vary by state. As a result, fundamental work is being done on how to construct appropriate policies and enforcement mechanisms in this space.

ARL research in trust places it in the context of developing capabilities for continuous monitoring and managing of vulnerabilities and risks in Army's highly heterogeneous networks such as C4ISR[10] networks and broader socio-technical networks. A key risk is the loss of trust in networks. To quantify and model the dynamics of trust in networks, ARL explores socio-cognitive models of trust for achieving fast trust emergence, propagation, and high sustainability. Potential benefits of algorithms based on such theories and models have been demonstrated already in several problems, such as routing of information through networks with nodes of different and uncertain levels of trustworthiness, and detection of cyber-compromise nodes by collaborative assessment of trust by multiple nodes in the network.

NIST's **Security Content Automation Protocol (SCAP) Program** is developing a common framework and language for specifying instructions for security configuration. The program began in response to the Cyber Security R&D Act of 2002 and has since grown to become a suite of specifications that standardize how security configuration information can be communicated to machines and humans. SCAP is capable of describing other security-related attributes and holds the promise of enabling and automating the characterization of Tailored Trustworthy Spaces. Similarly, the ONR **Fabric Project** will provide a software development environment for establishing security guarantees based on explicitly stated security policies.

Spotlight on ONR – *Fabric Project*	The **Fabric Project** supports the development of strong, principled, security guarantees based on explicitly stated security policies for distributed systems with complex, incomplete, and changing trust between participants. Fabric provides a software development environment to achieve strong security in federated systems, while giving programmers a simple, clear, high-level programming model that frees them from dealing with low-level implementation details. Fabric's platform and application development environment supports securely interconnecting distributed systems, code, and data from different trust domains. In this development environment, all

---

[10] Command, Control, Communications, Computers, Intelligence, Surveillance, Reconnaissance

information resources (code and data, both local and remote) look to the programmer like objects, and they are protected in a uniform way using an inherently compositional security mechanism and information flow control. Fabric is freely available, has been used as a teaching tool in many universities, and is being evaluated by government laboratories. The program began in FY 2009 and will continue until FY 2016.

5.1.2.2 Trust Negotiation

The area of Trust Negotiation focuses on frameworks, methods, and technologies to establish trust between system components based on articulated policies via dynamic human-understandable and machine-readable instructions. This requires being able to adjust the assurance level on specific security attributes separately, for example, to establish the differences between an anonymous, low assurance, or high assurance Tailored Trustworthy Space. Future uses of dynamic Tailored Trustworthy Spaces will also require the development of methods to tailor that space given a threat scenario.

Historically, trust negotiation is an area with substantial prior research, which now can be leveraged in the context of Tailored Trustworthy Spaces. Examples of current research in this domain include AFRL's **Trusted Hardware/Secure Processor Program**, which is developing hardware-based roots of trust; ARL's **Trust Management for Optimal Network Performance Program**, whose goal is to enhance distributed decision-making capabilities in the context of network-centric operations by understanding the role trust plays in networks that consist of large systems with complex interactions between communication, information, and social/cognitive networks; and DHS's **Hardware-Enabled Trust Program**.

Spotlight on DHS – *Digital Provenance and Hardware-Enabled Trust Programs*	DHS's **Digital Provenance and Hardware-Enabled Trust Programs** develop capabilities to determine the trustworthiness and reliability of data that could have originated from different sources and may have been transformed, processed, aggregated, or otherwise manipulated by many entities. The programs also develop hardware-enabled resilience against all forms of malicious activity. Specifically, the program is researching and developing a digital object tracking platform and tools to fulfill legal and regulatory requirements for evidentiary handling and chain of custody. Under these programs, DHS will develop an end-to-end trust architecture, demonstrate it using a combination of simulated hardware and system prototypes, and test its resilience against attack. Two awards were made in September 2012 under the DHS 2011 BAA and 2012 SBIR actions. Both projects are developing hardware-based malware defenses. In addition, the BAA work will contribute to hardware defense by developing radically new foundations for end-to-end trust, as well as protection against zero-day hardware exploits. As a result, the protected hardware will exhibit greater resilience and will function effectively, even while under attack.

5.1.2.3 Operations

There are a number of operations that are necessary for dynamic Tailored Trustworthy Spaces, including joining, dynamically tailoring, splitting, merging, and dismantling. These operations are necessary to sustain the "tailoring" of the trustworthy spaces on hand.

Within NSF, the **Secure and Trustworthy Cyberspace (SaTC) Program** funded 21 awards in the Tailored Trustworthy Spaces area in FY 2012, making this theme a significant portion of the SaTC portfolio. In general, there were two categories of such awards: work that establishes the base technology that allows systems to be tailored and specific applications of Tailored Trustworthy Spaces technology to specific environments. An example of the former is a project investigating network-defense systems that adaptively learn "normal" behavior in their deployed environment. One project in the latter group allows for secure and reliable communication across a network whose owner is untrustworthy.

Another example of research in Tailored Trustworthy Spaces operations is the IARPA **Automatic Privacy Protection (APP) Program**, which is developing techniques to provide options for tailoring privacy protection in cyberspace transactions. Additionally, DOE's **Bio-Inspired Technologies for Enhancing Cybersecurity Program** is developing new architectures for implementing cybersecurity policies tailored to different energy system domains.

Spotlight on DOE – *Bio-Inspired Technologies for Enhancing Cybersecurity Program*	The DOE **Bio-Inspired Technologies for Enhancing Cybersecurity Program** aims to develop Digital Ants, a biologically inspired cybersecurity solution, and demonstrate that Digital Ants can be successfully deployed across multiple organizational and technological domains found in the energy sector. Digital Ants are designed to leave digital trails in the computer networks whenever they find anomalies or cyber threats, which in turn attract other Ants. Such emergent behavior can dynamically define and adjust cybersecurity policies tailored to individual domains. The Digital Ants project has deployed the framework on multiple platforms and testbeds, from small embedded computers to large computer clusters. The framework has been exercised on up to 20,000 nodes, with plans to scale even larger. Future research will focus on human-assisted automation that will be suitable for utility control room operations.

5.1.2.4 Privacy

Privacy is an important individual and societal concern in the digital age. The ability to achieve and maintain appropriate modes of privacy in cyberspace is challenged by business innovations, rapid technological changes, and sometimes by unintended legal consequences. Cognizant of these challenges, the Federal Government has been a strong advocate of privacy in cyberspace. For example, the Administration's efforts include the President's framework for consumer data privacy.[11] One of the key elements that this framework recognizes is that privacy is dynamic and contextual; privacy determinations always depend on the context in which activities or information disclosures occur. The broader issue of privacy in cyberspace is discussed as a new priority area in Section 6.3.2.

The Tailored Trustworthy Spaces research theme serves as a framework for creating custom cyberspace environments that allow fine-grained control of environmental characteristics for establishing and

---

[11] "Consumer Data Privacy in a Networked World: a Framework for Protecting Privacy and Promoting Innovation in the Global Digital Economy," The White House, February 2012, http://www.whitehouse.gov/sites/default/files/privacy-final.pdf

enforcing desired security and privacy objectives. By tailoring an environment's characteristics and establishing policies for the activities and data encompassed by a Tailored Trustworthy Space (e. g., policies defining access control, identity management, attribution, etc.), the actors also establish the context in which interactions take place. This tailoring capability offers direct support for achieving desirable privacy conditions in cyberspace. One example of research in this area is the IARPA **Security and Privacy Assurance Research (SPAR) Program**, which aims to create practical solutions for secure and private data exchange.

Spotlight on IARPA – *Security and Privacy Assurance Research (SPAR) Program*	IARPA started the **Security and Privacy Assurance Research Program** in 2011, building on the success of the past IARPA Automatic Privacy Protection (APP) Program. The goal of the SPAR Program is to develop and demonstrate practical techniques for data exchange that protect the security and privacy interests of each exchanging party. The program has several phases and will end in FY 2014. The APP Program developed efficient cryptographic protocols for simple queries. The SPAR Program seeks to expand support to complex queries critical to mission applications, while retaining the efficiency demonstrated in the APP Program. SPAR is developing efficient means of protecting security and privacy to allow parties to share just the information that needs to be shared, without risking unnecessary disclosure of sensitive data. The capabilities will allow information access to be tailored to the privileges and need-to-know of parties in a much more granular way than ever before. The data exchange scenarios that will be addressed in the SPAR Program are: complex database queries, publish/subscribe systems, message queue/mailbox systems, and outsourced data storage systems.

5.1.3 Designed-In Security

The vision and goals of the Designed-In Security research theme are as follows:

Vision

Develop the capability to design, implement, and evolve software/hardware systems that are resistant to cyber-attacks, while effectively managing risk, quality, cost, schedule, and complexity. Provide assurance evidence necessary to attest to the level of confidence in the system's ability to withstand attacks.

Goals

- Using assurance-focused engineering practices, languages, and tools, provide the capability to design software systems that are resistant to attacks by dramatically reducing exploitable flaws

- Improve the usability of tools for specifying, implementing, analyzing, and testing attack-resistant software and hardware systems

- Develop the capability to reason about a diversity of assurance attributes (security, safety, reliability, etc.) and the evidence required to achieve the desired confidence in a system's resistance to attacks

Establishing and maintaining the security (confidentiality, integrity, availability, authentication, non-repudiation) of computer systems has been an objective of the computing field since its inception. Security theory and modeling have evolved in concert with advancements in computing hardware, operating systems, programming languages, and software development methodologies. Foundations for security in computing were put in place in the 1960s and 1970s and were supported by parallel developments in areas such as programming methodologies, program verification, and automated theorem proving. Subsequent interdisciplinary concerns in risk management, privacy, regulatory and standards compliance, and disaster recovery gave rise to information assurance as a field with broader security concerns.

The legacy of security advancements in computing, information assurance, and software assurance has produced many point-solutions, for example, in code analysis or best practices in secure coding. These solutions are valuable, but their effects are limited as the solutions do not scale up to enable capabilities that would allow us to comprehensively design and maintain systems that are resistant to cyber-attacks. Consequently, Federally funded research in Designed-In Security gives priority to achieving progress in the following areas:

- Software development and verification environments

- Assurance evidence and synthesis

- Design tools

5.1.3.1 Software Development and Verification Environments

This area of research creates integrated, security-aware software development environments that can automatically recognize and identify vulnerabilities in code, suggest corrections for identified vulnerabilities, and generate software without code-based vulnerabilities. This area includes research in methods for detecting flaws in software (e.g., formal methods, static or dynamic analysis techniques), improved development tools, such as source code compilers with automatic insertion of constructs that guarantee security and robustness of codes written in unsecured languages, and methods that automatically capture and utilize work flow and design decisions during software coding to aid in the development of functioning systems that meet performance and security requirements.

One focus within these areas is integrating tools into comprehensive development environments that support and assure software design and maintenance across a wide range of security requirements. For example, one of the NSF **SaTC Program** awards in Designed-In Security, titled "High-Level Language Support for Trustworthy Networks," is developing new network programming languages that give programmers the ability to specify what a network should do, separate from how it will be implemented, together with modular constructs that facilitate compositional reasoning about programs. The goal of the project is to transform the way that networks are built by developing network-wide, correct-by-construction programming abstractions and verification tools based on rigorous semantic foundations.

A key feature of security-aware software development and verification environments is usability. The ONR **Software Efficiency Reclamation Program** focuses on enhancing security while also reducing programming complexity through a number of automated processes.

Spotlight on ONR – *Software Efficiency Reclamation Program*	The ONR **Software Efficiency Reclamation Program** provides a novel approach for enhancing software execution security and efficiency while preserving programmers' productivity by reducing unnecessary complexity introduced by software development practices. It focuses on reclaiming

software execution efficiency by reducing indirection and performing automatic program de-layering and specialization, such that the result is compact and efficient code/executable, with much reduced attack surface and more modest computing resource and energy requirements. This program directly addresses and reduces one of the root causes of software system vulnerability—the complexity of the software. The Software Efficiency Reclamation program was initiated in FY 2013 and will run through FY 2016. It is anticipated that this program will provide a new alternative for deploying software that will allow software customization (for reducing complexity) at installation or pre-execution time, resulting in software that is both more secure and more efficient. The desired contributions of this program are advancements in binary analysis, binary rewriting, program slicing, and program optimization.

5.1.3.2   Assurance Evidence and Synthesis

Assurance evidence and synthesis is a foundational area with the objective of developing systems with provable security properties by achieving a synthesis of system functional specifications, safety and security policies, resource constraints, hardware specifications, and operational environmental descriptions. Key to this effort is the challenge of developing formal methods and models for component architectures that produce desirable safety and security properties in composition with one another. Provable system security properties must be supported by verifiable assurance evidence that is inextricably linked with the system design and can be maintained with the system through its lifecycle. DARPA's **High-Assurance Cyber Military Systems (HACMS) Program** is an example of research in this area, with the objective of achieving automated code synthesis from executable, formal system requirements that include security specifications.

Spotlight on DARPA – *High-Assurance Cyber Military Systems (HACMS) Program*	DARPA's **High-Assurance Cyber Military Systems Program** aims to create technology for the construction of high-assurance cyber-physical systems via a clean-slate, formal methods-based approach that enables semi-automated code synthesis from executable, formal specifications. High assurance is defined to mean both functionally correct and satisfying appropriate safety and security properties. Achieving this goal requires a fundamentally different approach from what the software community has taken to date. In addition to a code generator, HACMS seeks a synthesizer capable of producing a machine-checkable proof that assures that the generated code satisfies functional specifications as well as security and safety policies. A key technical challenge is the development of techniques to ensure that the proofs can be composed, allowing the construction of high-assurance systems out of high-assurance components.

5.1.3.3   Design Tools

Tools and the usability of tools for designing secure systems continue to be important areas of research as components of integrated development environments and as instruments for obtaining assurance evidence. The **Secure Coding Initiative (SCI)** at the Software Engineering Institute (SEI) at Carnegie Mellon University, supported by OSD funding, is an example of the development of secure coding standards and supporting tools, such as compilers for the C/C++ programming language. The DOE **Secure Coding for Energy Control Systems Initiative** is leveraging the work done by SEI in secure code development to refine it for use in energy control and delivery systems. Another example is the **Model-Based Evaluation of System Dependability and Security (Mobius) Program**, funded in part by DHS and DOE, which is developing a toolset that combines attacker, system, and user modeling formalisms, as well as probabilistic evaluation and model composition to allow broad exploration of the system design space for best satisfaction of security requirements.

5.1.4 Cyber Economic Incentives

The vision and goals of the Cyber Economic Incentives research theme are as follows:

Vision

Promote understanding of cyber economic incentives by creating a science-based understanding of markets, decision making, and motivators; promote an environment where deployment of security technology is balanced, providing incentives to engage in responsible behavior and deter criminal and malicious behavior.

Goals

- Develop theories and models of cyber economics and scientific understanding of the social and behavioral dimensions of cybersecurity

- Explore economic models of cybersecurity investments and markets

- Define meaningful cybersecurity metrics and support the collection of cyberspace data (e.g., usage, incidents, attacks, losses) to enable economic, financial, social, and behavioral analyses

A key objective of the Strategic Plan is to achieve breakthroughs that induce positive changes in cyberspace. The Cyber Economic Incentives research theme aims to induce fundamental changes in cyberspace through economic incentives, broadly encompassing costs and benefits (monetary and otherwise), as well as their allocation, liabilities, and analyses. Without good metrics, processes that enable assured development, sensible and enforceable notions of liability, and mature cost risk analysis methods, the allocation of resources for security will be distorted. Research is needed to develop a sound basis for the economic and social incentives that promote good cybersecurity practices and discourage cybercrime and other bad behavior, and that benefit individuals, organizations, and the larger public good.

As a market, cyberspace suffers from the same inefficiencies observed in other sectors. Some of these inefficiencies include externalities, information asymmetries, and framing effects. Understanding the economic (as well as the social and behavioral) relationships and interactions in cyberspace is a necessary step in facilitating appropriate incentives and enabling effective business decisions to engage in responsible cybersecurity practices.

NSF is at the forefront of Federal research in economic, social, and behavioral influences on cyberspace. Since its FY 2011 **Secure and Trustworthy Cyberspace (SaTC) Program** solicitation, NSF has explicitly supported research in "economic incentives, cybersecurity investments, markets, and motivators." The SaTC Program includes funding for research on the psychological and sociological aspects of cybersecurity decisions and incentives; metrics and data for evaluating and understanding security; behavioral economic analyses of privacy decision making; motivators of insider threat and incentive countermeasures; impacts of trust and institutional design on cybersecurity decisions; incentive structures for cybersecurity in firms and other organizations; and behavioral aspects of real-world vulnerability markets and associated insurance/software-derivative instruments. This program is laying the foundation for research in cyber economics by explicitly funding multidisciplinary investigations that bring together computer science, economics, and behavioral sciences researchers. In FY 2012, SaTC funded 18 Cyber-Economic Incentive awards, making this theme a significant portion of the SaTC portfolio. Topics of these awards included understanding the malware economy, understanding how to deter malicious activities, and pricing strategies for Smart Grid systems that cause the systems to stabilize.

DHS, through its 2011 BAA, has initiated a **Cyber Economics Incentives Program** to develop new theories and models of cyber economics and a scientific understanding of the social dimensions of cyber economics. This program will reexamine scientific frameworks to incentivize vendors of cyberspace-related technologies (e.g., encourage use of secure software engineering and analysis practices, and software vulnerability detection) and security incident forensics through acquisition, regulation, and standards.

In addition to the broader cyber economic programs implemented by NSF and DHS, agencies have implemented targeted research programs focusing on studying the details of the economic models behind security challenges of particular concern; for example, ONR is conducting in-depth research on the underground economies supporting botnets.

Spotlight on ONR – *Infiltration of Botnet Command-and-Control and Support Ecosystems Project through the Multidisciplinary University Research Initiative (MURI)*	The ONR **Infiltration of Botnet Command-and-Control and Support Ecosystems** project through the **Multidisciplinary University Research Initiative (MURI)** was started in FY 2009 with the objective of increasing our understanding of cyberspace underground economics and to provide insights on how to curb some of the activities. In addition to exploring the economics behind the cyberspace underground, the program is investigating techniques for infiltration of botnet command and control structures, for automated analysis of malware binaries, and applications of natural-language processing to gain insights from human communications that support the botnet ecosystem. The program is scheduled for completion in FY 2014.

5.2 Developing Scientific Foundations

The research themes within the Inducing Change thrust focus on near-term threats and current or near-horizon challenges and technologies. In addition to these efforts, the Federal Government must also provide investments for laying the theoretical, empirical, computational, and data mining foundations needed to meet needs arising from next-generation technologies and to address the threats of the future. Developing a strong, rigorous scientific foundation to cybersecurity helps the field in the following ways:

- **Organizes disparate areas of knowledge**: Provides structure and organization to a broad-based body of knowledge in the form of testable models and predictions

- **Enables discovery of universal laws**: Produces laws that express an understanding of basic, universal dynamics against which to test problems and formulate explanations

- **Applies the rigor of the scientific method**: Approaches problems using a systematic methodology and discipline to formulate hypotheses, design and execute repeatable experiments, and collect and analyze data

5.2.1 Foundations for Science of Security

Agencies have already begun support for research aimed at developing a cyber-science base, or "a science of security." Programs within a growing group of agencies are now providing funding for research on difficult scientific problems, such as system composition and measurement, as well as supporting the formation of a community of practice centered upon the creation of a scientific base.

The Air Force Office of Scientific Research (AFOSR), ARL, NSA, and NSF have a coordinated Science of Security effort underway. In FY 2010, AFOSR, NSA, and NSF developed a set of research objectives to advance the science of security and then supported these objectives by funding several related research projects. Later, in FY 2011, AFOSR awarded a five-year-long MURI on the "**Science of Cyber Security Modeling, Composition, and Measurement**." The purpose of this MURI is to advance the scientific basis for trustworthiness by developing concepts, relationships, and laws with predictive value that focus on security modeling, composition, and measurement. Complementary to these activities, ARL has a **Science for Cyber** portfolio focused on developing novel theoretical constructs that can enable future cybersecurity advances. Programs in the portfolio explore models for the representation of cybersecurity, ensemble techniques for improved detection of attacks, and behavior as a fundamental indicator in detection and analysis. In particular, the research program focuses on theories and models that will lead to more effective intrusion detection techniques.

In February 2014, NSA awarded four universities with funding to create four "science of security" research centers, which are termed "lablets." The lablets will jump-start multidisciplinary, multifaceted collaborative research in five key areas of security: scalability and composability, policy governed secure collaboration, predictive security metrics, resilient architectures, and human behavior and usability. Because there are many possible and different paths towards creating a security science, early stages of this work will be directed at exploring a wide variety of methods and building a large community to support this field.

Public comments have stressed that the Strategic Plan should include greater exploration of the role that the field of cryptographic design can play in addressing the central challenges of cybersecurity. Advances in cryptography (e.g., fully homomorphic encryption) will continue to play an important role in the building of fundamentally secure cyber solutions. Research activities in both the Designed-In Security theme and Developing Scientific Foundations thrust reflect the need for and importance of research on rigorous and formal foundations for achieving security. In FY 2012, 35 of NSF's SaTC awards focused on advancing the foundations of the field, with theoretical cryptography representing a large portion of the awards made. Other topics of research included programming language semantics that specifically seek to capture security-related behavior, cloud computing on encrypted data, and methods for incorporating real world data into scientific security research in a way that respects privacy concerns. For example, NSF SaTC awards for a project called Critter@Home, inspired by SETI@Home, allow individual computer users to gather security information that can be queried in a distributed but privacy-preserving manner, allowing researchers to find out what is happening at end-user computers in near real time. Since the raw data never leaves the individual's computer, many privacy issues are avoided.

Spotlight on NSF –

Secure and Trustworthy Cyberspace (SaTC) Program

In strong alignment with the themes outlined in the Strategic Plan, the NSF SaTC program's approach to research, development, and education leverages the disciplines of mathematics and statistics, the social, behavioral, and economic sciences, and engineering together with the computing, communications, and information sciences. Spanning NSF's Directorates for Computer and Information Science and Engineering (CISE), Education and Human Resources (EHR), Engineering (ENG), Mathematical and Physical Sciences (MPS), and Social, Behavioral & Economic Sciences (SBE), the multidisciplinary SaTC portfolio currently comprises approximately 650 active awards that range from seedling grants (typically around $150K/18 months) to large-scale, multi-institution *Frontier* awards (up to $10M/5 years). The **Frontier awards** SaTC awarded in FY 2013 were:

The **Rethinking Security in the Era of Cloud Computing** project, dubbed Project Silver and led by University of North Carolina at Chapel Hill, seeks to exploit the opportunities inherent in leveraging cloud providers as trusted partners to improve tenant security. The project convenes periodic "Cloud Security Horizons" summits with industry stakeholders to help shape the future of security in the cloud.

The **Trustworthy Health and Wellness** (THaW) project led by Dartmouth College includes experts from computer science, business, behavioral health, health policy, and healthcare information technology. The project is tackling the challenges of providing trustworthy information systems for health and wellness given that sensitive information and health-related tasks are being increasingly pushed to mobile devices and cloud-based services.

The **Usable Privacy Policy Project** led by Carnegie Mellon University is developing scalable technologies for extracting key privacy policy features semi-automatically from website privacy policies, thereby helping users understand the privacy provided by websites before disclosing their information. This project includes transitioning their technology into open source browsers.

During FY 2013 and FY 2014, SaTC initiated a series of seedling grants seeking to catalyze new collaborations between computer scientists and social scientists, with the goal of increasing the pool of interdisciplinary research. Among the topics being explored by the inaugural set of grants in FY 2013 are frameworks for Moving Target defense, using new visualization methods to improve passwords, user-tailored privacy and security systems, and assessing cybercrime vulnerability.

FY 2013 also marked the addition of the EHR Directorate to the SaTC solicitation, and 12 new cybersecurity education research projects were funded. Among these are a healthcare-based cybersecurity competition designed to bring young women into the field; a "build it, break it, fix it" competition to encourage not just breaking into, but also improving systems; a cybersecurity education center targeted toward veterans; and an effort focused on curriculum development for cyber-physical systems security and privacy education.

In addition to the initiatives described previously, which are broader-scoped explorations of the scientific foundations of security, agencies, such as AFRL, have also created programs and solicitations that explore foundational research in security with the end goal of supporting their explicit mission needs.

Spotlight on AFRL – *Cyber Assurance Technologies Solicitation*	Many of the research projects for the AFRL "Invent Foundations of Trust and Assurance" strategic objective are funded through the AFRL **Cyber Assurance Technologies Solicitation** issued in FY 2011. "Invent Foundations of Trust and Assurance" is one of AFRL's four primary strategic goals for cybersecurity research. The end goal of this strategy is to provide the Air Force with capabilities to mitigate supply chain intervention and to establish hardware and software roots-of-trust; to create the foundations of trust for applications, functions, and missions; and to develop the mathematical algebra to represent missions, applications, and infrastructure for provably correct mission characterizations in contested environments. AFRL will use a scientific characterization of cyberinfrastructure relative to mission functionality and criticality to focus and prioritize the efforts toward developing assured, verifiable, and trusted hardware and software.

5.2.2 Metrics, Models, and Experiments

Cybersecurity metrics make up another major area of interest in agency programs supporting the science of security. Multiple public comments highlighted cybersecurity metrics as a key area for foundational research and development. Currently, two major research activities are underway that focus on cybersecurity metrics: the OSD **Cyber Measurement Campaign (CMC)** and the DOE **Cyber-Physical Survivability Metrics Program**. The DOE program seeks to develop a suite of metrics and models for assessing, comparing, and gaining actionable insight into the cyber-physical survivability properties of large-scale, highly networked energy delivery systems. The metrics and models will provide the capabilities to evaluate, quantify, and improve the survivability of existing delivery systems and to engineer new systems that exhibit the intended survivability properties in the context of explicit engineering tradeoffs.

Spotlight on OSD – *Cyber Measurement Campaign (CMC)*	OSD's **Cyber Measurement Campaign** was launched in August 2011 and is scheduled to continue until FY 2015. The end goal of the campaign is to develop a suite of metrics to define hypothesis-driven experiments that measure key cybersecurity capabilities. There are three aspects to the CMC: Cyber Technology Measurement, Cyber Range Fidelity Measurement, and Experimental Infrastructure. Initial experiments focus on quantifying cyber-resiliency with mature research prototypes, as well as measuring resulting improvements to cybersecurity. For example, one of the initial experiments already conducted tested the hypothesis that increasing an attacker's uncertainty increases workload. The test used ARCSYNE technology to create an IP hopping defense in a closed community of interest. The results showed a dramatic increase in the time and workload required to execute a successful attack. So far, simple scenarios have been used to generate initial results. Growth into complex operational scenarios with realistic settings will enable the derivation of general models and metrics.

5.3 Maximizing Research Impact

Maximizing the impact of research outlined in the game-changing R&D themes will require cooperation between government and private sector communities, collaboration across international borders, integration of output across research themes, and the support of national priorities such as health IT and Smart Grid systems. As President Obama said in May 2009, "America's economic prosperity in the 21st century will depend on cybersecurity."

5.3.1 Integrating Research Efforts and Engaging the Research Community

DoD OSD's **Cyber Applied Research and Advanced Development Program** supports integration across multiple cybersecurity research themes. This program funds DoD laboratories and the NSA to develop technological solutions that can be applied across cyber operations. This research effort enhances and extends the work of individual laboratories and encourages cross-laboratory collaboration.

To facilitate exchange and collaboration by the broader scientific cyber research community and to support peer-reviewed research communities in areas not served by mainstream organizations, the Office of the Director of National Intelligence (ODNI) has created a new **Journal of Sensitive Cybersecurity Research and Engineering (JSCoRE)**. The new journal allows the secure dissemination of peer-reviewed, high-quality, and sensitive cybersecurity research to governmental, commercial, and academic communities with appropriate security clearance accesses.

A number of workshops are organized by agencies to engage the research community. Some examples include the DHS Cybersecurity Applications and Technology Conference for Homeland Security, DHS/DoD Small Business Innovation Research (SBIR) Conference, DHS/NIST/NSA Annual IT Security Automation Conference, DHS/NIST/NSA/NSF/OSD National Initiative for Cybersecurity Education Annual Workshop, DHS/GSA/NIST Cloud Forums, NIST/NSA Mobile Security Forum, NSF Workshops on Incorporating Security Concepts in Undergraduate Computer Science Curriculum, NSF Workshop on Multi-spectrum Metrics for Cyber Defense, NSF/National Laboratories Workshop on the Human Dimensions in Cyber Operations R&D Priorities, DHS/NSF Cybersecurity Insurance Workshop, DHS IT Security Entrepreneur Forum, Innovation Summit, SINET Showcase, and Transition To Practice Showcase, NSA Science of Security Workshop, DHS/DOE Trustworthy Cyber Infrastructure for the Power Grid (TCIPG) Industry Workshops, and ODNI Workshops on Computational Cybersecurity in Compromised Environments.

Supporting the development of technical standards is another area of how agencies collaborate with industry. For example, NIST and NSA have been developing, maintaining, and coordinating validation programs for cryptographic standards; NIST, NSA, and OSD participate in Internet Engineering Task Force (IETF) security groups to develop standard representations and corresponding reference implementations of security-relevant data; and NIST and DOE/OE support the development of Smart Grid standards through the Smart Grid Interoperability Panel (SGIP) Cyber Security Working Group (CSWG).

In addition to domestic programs, Federal research agencies support and fund collaborative cybersecurity R&D with a number of international partners. Public comments have noted that there are a host of cybersecurity R&D-related issues that must be discussed in an international context, including how international efforts in innovative technologies impact the development of the U.S. cybersecurity efforts; and how international technical requirements affect American companies, create trade barriers, and impact public procurement practices. We note that the U.S. *International Strategy for Cyberspace*[12]

---

[12] http://www.whitehouse.gov/sites/default/files/rss_viewer/international_strategy_for_cyberspace.pdf

defines the strategic and policy objectives for the U.S. Government in engaging international partners on a range of cyber issues. This strategy will also guide cybersecurity R&D efforts that engage international partners or stakeholders.

The DoD has a number of international partnerships such as **The Technical Cooperation Program (TTCP)**. TTCP is a 50-year-old military R&D Memorandum of Understanding among the countries of Australia, Canada, New Zealand, the United Kingdom, and the United States designed to support cooperation on research to reduce duplication of effort and maximize mutual benefits. The Command, Control, Communications, and Information Systems (C3I) Group within TTCP addresses technologies to achieve interoperable, seamless information systems focused on the support of allied military missions. Technical Panel 11 focuses on the areas of information assurance and defensive information warfare.

Other DoD international partnerships include the Network and Information Sciences **International Technology Alliance (ITA)**, a collaborative research alliance between the UK Ministry of Defense (UK MoD) and ARL, and a consortium of leading academic and industry partners. Now in its seventh year, ITA continues to support research on secure data sharing and collaboration among coalition partners. In 2010, ONR's Global Division opened a new international science and technology office in Prague, Czech Republic. The Prague office established a regional presence for the U.S. Navy within the eastern Europe international science and technology community. The Czech-ONR Global relationship includes joint research in a number of cyber technologies, such as Multi Agent Systems (with a focus on adversarial reasoning, distributed control systems, and distributed computing).

Further strengthening international engagements, DHS has initiated jointly funded projects with U.S. partners. Currently, Australia, UK, Canada, the Netherlands, Sweden, Germany, and Israel co-fund projects within the DHS S&T 2011 Cyber BAA. Additionally, NSF supports collaborative research in computer science and cybersecurity between researchers in the U.S. and Israel through the United States-Israel Binational Science Foundation (BSF).

In November 2006 and April 2007, two International Cooperation in Trustworthy, Secure and Dependable ICT Infrastructures (INCO-TRUST) workshops were held with researchers from the EU, US, Australia, Japan, and Canada who engaged within ICT Trust, Security and Dependability. These workshops were highly successful in their mission of identifying and scoping research areas that require and will benefit from international collaboration between EU researchers and those within other industrialized nations.[13] More recently, out of the connections that were established through INCO-TRUST, NSF Principal Investigators have participated in the European Union's Building International Cooperation for Trustworthy ICT (BIC) project.

5.3.2 Supporting National Priorities

The 2011 Strategic Plan outlined several activities already underway at agencies that targeted national priorities with substantial cybersecurity influences. Since the release of the Plan, several agencies have expanded on these cybersecurity tracks and started new programs that focus on applied cybersecurity research in national priority fields.[14]

---

[13] DHS and NSF both were sponsors of these workshops, and their PIs participated. The workshop reports for these events are available at http://www.inco-trust.eu/incotrust/general/project-motivation.html.

[14] While this section outlines some cybersecurity R&D activities geared towards specific national priorities, not all end uses require specialized lines of research. Some public comments push for creation of new lines of cybersecurity research for specific end uses, such as law enforcement and defense purposes. However, the Strategic Plan already supports research on these types of areas. For example, the Tailored Trustworthy Systems theme includes having security appropriate for the transaction at hand. The Moving Target theme recognizes that additional research may be necessary to satisfy the needs of cyber law enforcement in the context of "moving" system adaptations.

Privacy and security concerns must be satisfied in the use of valuable health information. The **Strategic Healthcare IT Advanced Research Projects on Security (SHARPS) Program** of the Office of the National Coordinator for Health Information Technology (ONC) focuses on advancing the requirements, foundations, design, development and deployment of security, privacy tools, and methods for electronic health records, health information exchanges, and telemedicine. For example, the SHARPS Program is applying state-of-the-art techniques in encryption, ciphertext policy, and decryption based on biomarkers to safeguard data transmitted by electronic health record systems and health information exchanges. Complementary to SHARPS is NIST's **Health IT Security Program**, which focuses on solutions that enable interoperability and adoption of health IT technologies. For example, using security automation specifications (a research area within Tailored Trustworthy Spaces), the Health IT Security Program accelerates the deployment of health IT platforms by enabling automated security certification to Health Insurance Portability and Accountability Act (HIPAA) regulations.

NIST also initiated and chaired the Smart Grid Interoperability Panel Cybersecurity Committee (SGCC), which led the collaboration between the private sector, academia, national research laboratories, and Federal agencies in facilitating the development of cybersecurity standards for the Smart Grid. For example, similar to NIST's work in Health IT and cybersecurity, SGCC developed the NISTIR 7628, "Guidelines for Smart Grid Cybersecurity," which is being used globally as a foundational tool for helping to secure the Smart Grid. In January 2013, the Smart Grid Interoperability Panel (SGIP) fully transitioned to a private/public partnership funded by industry stakeholders in cooperation with the Federal Government. NIST continues to have an active role in SGIP. Current news and member information now reside at http://www.sgip.org/.

Similarly, DOE research efforts advancing the goals of the 2011 Roadmap to Achieve Energy Delivery Systems Cybersecurity[15] utilize multiple Tailored Trustworthy Spaces concepts. These efforts include SIEGate, an information exchange gateway that provides secure data communication between control centers; Secure and Real-time Communication Substrate, a trustworthy cyber infrastructure and technologies for wide-area monitoring, control, and active energy demand management; and Trust Anchors, which are monitoring and control devices that independently verify systems function, reveal deceptive malicious function, attest to system state, and verify correctness of system tests. The alignment of Tailored Trustworthy Spaces and cybersecurity R&D in the energy sector was explored at the NITRD Workshop on Tailored Trustworthy Spaces: Solutions for the Smart Grid on July 2011 in Washington, DC.

NSF's SaTC Program supports security research related to many of the cyber-physical systems that make up the critical infrastructure supporting multiple national priority areas, such as biomedical devices, the Smart Grid, transportation systems, and environment monitoring. SaTC also supports the Administration's focus on education by funding the NSF **CyberCorps: Scholarship for Service Program**, which sustains efforts to establish curricula for new courses, degree programs, and pathways in cybersecurity education. Public comments on the Strategic Plan have emphasized the importance of training: the Plan and associated research must include training and the training should integrate the results of research to help the workforce adopt new technologies and practices.

---

[15] http://energy.gov/sites/prod/files/Energy%20Delivery%20Systems%20Cybersecurity%20Roadmap_finalweb.pdf

Spotlight on NSF –

CyberCorps®:
Scholarships for Service

The goal of the **CyberCorps®: Scholarship for Service (SFS) Program**, administered by NSF and supported by the Office of Personnel Management and DHS, is to educate, recruit, and retain the next generation of cybersecurity professionals. NSF issues grants to colleges and universities for student scholarships in support of education in areas relevant to cybersecurity. In return for their scholarships, recipients agree to work after graduation for the Federal Government, a State, Local, or Tribal government in a position related to cybersecurity for a period equal to the length of the scholarship.

As of April 2014, there were 51 SFS scholarship institutions with more than 460 active scholarships awarded to undergraduate and graduate students. The first SFS graduates entered the Federal workforce in 2002 and since then over 2,000 students (24% bachelors, 73% masters, and 3% doctoral degrees) have been admitted to the SFS program with 1536 completing their degrees. SFS scholarship recipients have been placed in internships and full-time positions in more than 120 Federal agencies and departments, including the NSA, the CIA, and the Departments of Defense, Treasury, Commerce, Homeland Security, and Justice as well as in State, Local, or Tribal governments. The overall placement rate of the SFS program is 93 percent.

The top enrolling SFS institution has been the University of Tulsa where each student is assigned to a Tulsa police crime lab on campus to perform forensics on digital devices. In 2003, SFS students contributed to a triple homicide investigation by tracing email communication from victims to the perpetrator. Another unique feature of the Tulsa program is the presence of the U.S. Secret Service facility on campus where SFS students have collaborated with U.S. Secret Service agents to develop new ways for recovering data from more than 5,000 damaged cellphones, GPS, and other devices.

5.4 Accelerating Transition to Practice

An explicit, coordinated process that transitions the fruits of research into practice is essential if Federal cybersecurity R&D investments are to have significant, long-lasting impacts. Currently, a chasm exists between the research community, which focuses on exercising research components in demonstration environments, and the operations community, which acquires system prototypes containing research components and implements them in operational environments. Bridging that chasm, colloquially referred to as the "valley of death," requires cooperative efforts and investments by both the R&D and operations communities, and may involve risk-taking on the part of the private sector as it shepherds research results through the commercialization process. The Strategic Plan called out the need to have activities around discovering technology; testing and evaluation; and transition, adoption, and commercialization.

5.4.1 A Platform for Transitioning Research to Practice

In February 2012, DHS S&T initiated the **Transition to Practice (TTP) Program** with the mission of identifying promising federally funded cybersecurity research that can be transitioned to the private sector for commercialization in 24-36 months. DHS is partnering with agencies across the Federal R&D

community, focusing on the DOE national labs in FY 2012 to identify eight mature technologies that address existing or imminent cybersecurity gaps in public or private systems impacting national security. The TTP Program funds test and evaluation, red-teaming, pilots, and incremental improvements to research technologies, thereby filling an incubator role that has been lacking in the transition of Federal R&D. Additionally, the program may assist in funding the commercialization efforts of technologies that have successful test and evaluation, red-teaming, and pilot deployments. In FY 2013, TTP hosted the first annual Federal Government Technology Demonstration Day to showcase the eight technologies identified in FY 2012, and began the process toward building pilots based on these technologies. TTP also hosted a Technology Demonstration Day for the finance sector to attract pilot partners in this area of critical infrastructure, along with Investor, Integrator and IT Company Forums in Washington, D.C. and Silicon Valley to showcase the technologies and attract commercialization partners. Public comments have stressed that successful and efficient transition to practice requires dialogue between the 'suppliers' and 'customers' of the research, i.e., between university and laboratory researchers and industry technologists.

The OSD ASD(R&E) Cyber Transition to Practice (CTP) initiative focuses on moving cyber S&T into DoD operations, i.e., overcoming the well-known "valley of death" for S&T. Transitioning cyber S&T is challenging because it is typically software intensive, exhibits cross-cutting dependencies, inhabits a rapidly evolving landscape, and is immature when it emerges from laboratory R&D efforts. The CTP initiative matures and transitions cyber S&T through range-based test and evaluation, operational pilots, and SBIR phase 2E projects. The CTP initiative is focusing initially on DoD Laboratories, Federally Funded Research and Development Centers (FFRDC), and University Affiliated Research Centers (UARC) as sources of cyber S&T to transition to combatant commands, the DoD Services, and other government agencies.

Addressing the "valley of death" between academic research results and commercialization, the NSF SaTC Program includes a Transition to Practice perspective that provides funding for later phases of a research and development lifecycle, including applied research, prototyping, experimental deployment, and early adoption activities. In addition to the broader transition to practice programs listed above, there are a variety of activities that focus on transfer models for technologies that improve the security of currently deployed infrastructure and products, some of which are listed in the following section. Another mechanism for engagement of industry is the NSF Industry/University Cooperative Research Center (I/UCRC) Program: NSF supports a center called the Security & Software Engineering Research Center (S2ERC) that focuses on promoting industry and academic collaboration in the areas of security and software engineering. This center currently includes Ball State University, Iowa State University, and Virginia Polytechnic Institute, and is growing.

As a counterpoint, public comments have noted that academia is motivated today by disruptive technology transfer models where game-changing ideas can be commercialized with relatively small amounts of investment through start-up companies, and that technology transfer models are needed where solutions can be integrated into existing industry products and services for sustaining impact.

5.4.2 Unique Paths for Differing Technologies

Several agencies have also started broader transition to practice programs that encompass all aspects of the Accelerating Transition to Practice thrust, but have focused on certain types of technologies or on technologies with similar, but unique characteristics for implementation. For example, the AFRL **Next-Generation Cyber Warriors Initiative** selects, educates, trains, and augments cyber warriors for superior performance. The goal of this initiative is to develop and transition the technologies and identify the human skill sets needed to address key technical challenge areas related to optimizing our future cyber warriors: visualization, skill-augmentation, cyber education, and training.

NIST established the **National Cybersecurity Center of Excellence (NCCoE)** through a partnership with the State of Maryland and Montgomery County. The NCCoE is dedicated to furthering innovation through the rapid identification, integration, and adoption of practical, standards-based cybersecurity solutions. The center provides an environment that encourages interaction among businesses and solution providers, increases opportunities for innovation, and advances the current understanding of cybersecurity technology capabilities and costs. Initial focus areas include healthcare information exchanges and securing assets for the financial services sector. The NCCoE is also advancing building blocks of cybersecurity solutions that are applicable across multiple industry sectors.

DARPA and NSA have created programs that act as platforms for producing cybersecurity technologies with rapid turnaround times. In FY 2013, DARPA operated the **Cyber Fast Track (CFT) Program**, to build cybersecurity capabilities on an agile, quick-response basis, and to fund smaller cyber projects that result in rapid development of cyber technologies with potential for large payoffs. NSA's **Applied Research Prototypes Program** is designed to facilitate new industry engagements by funding short-turnaround cybersecurity technology R&D, with demonstrable prototypes delivered within three months of project initiation.

6 Assessing the Federal Response to the Strategic Plan

This section provides an analysis of the Federal response to the 2011 Strategic Plan and suggestions for additional areas of emphasis and research that are needed to adapt to broader changes in the cybersecurity landscape. Section 6.1 examines the sufficiency of the Federal response to the Strategic Plan, analyzing where overlap and gaps exist in current R&D activities. The analysis is based on NITRD coordination activities, agency feedback, and public comments. Section 6.2 lists technology areas that are currently within the scope of the Strategic Plan, but could benefit from additional emphasis. Section 6.3 describes two new major research areas for the Strategic Plan.

The analysis in Sections 6.2 and 6.3 considers public comments and whether ongoing research adequately supports Administration positions and initiatives established since publication of the Strategic Plan, including:

- The Administration's five priority areas of action for cybersecurity:
  - Protect Critical Infrastructure
  - Improve Incident Reporting and Response
  - Secure Federal Networks
  - Engage Internationally
  - Shape the Future
- Executive Order 13636 (EO 13636) "Improving Critical Infrastructure Cybersecurity"
- Presidential Policy Directive 21 (PPD-21) "Critical Infrastructure Security and Resilience"
- The Administration's goals for cybersecurity legislation

6.1 Sufficiency of the Federal Response

Overall, each thrust and theme has multiagency participation and support. While many programs address similar scientific thematic areas, the key areas of those programs are shaped by the unique mission needs of the different agencies. For example, even though NSF, NIST, and AFRL have each implemented Transition to Practice programs, NSF's program focuses on transitioning academic research results to commercialization; NIST's program fosters deployment and adoption of tools to enhance consumer confidence in IT systems; and AFRL trains cyber warriors in newly developed cybersecurity technologies.

The R&D outlined in the 2011 Strategic Plan is well-matched by agency efforts, with relatively few gaps and little overlap, given the overall level of Federal funding of cybersecurity R&D. One area of R&D that could benefit from additional emphasis is the Cyber Economic Incentives theme. Both DHS and NSF offer broadly scoped research programs in this area, which have contributed to progress in fundamental research. However, as with ONR's research on botnets, other agencies may benefit from activities that rigorously examine the economic basis of specific cyber threats that align with their missions.

6.2 Technology Areas for Additional Emphasis

The Strategic Plan's R&D framework encompasses a broad set of research topics and technologies. Since its introduction at the end of 2011, the Plan has elicited comments from the public, inputs from other Federal reports and strategy documents, and responses from agency experts. These inputs have guided the identification of research topics that could benefit from additional, specific emphasis.

6.2.1 Within Moving Target

6.2.1.1 Situational Awareness and Cyber Instrumentation
Situational awareness is critical in order to understand the current state in a network or system and to determine appropriate courses of action. Without situational awareness, real-time critical asset management cannot take place effectively. Situational awareness is made possible by cyber instrumentation, which provides the core underlying technology by which the diverse mechanisms and strategies that increase system resiliency and agility are measured. If the network or a system is not adequately instrumented, it is difficult to determine the effectiveness of a technology in either avoiding or resisting an attack and in adjusting active responses in near real-time.

6.2.2 Within Tailored Trustworthy Spaces

6.2.2.1 Roots of Trust
Modern computing devices consist of various hardware and software components at multiple layers of abstraction. Existing security measurement and protection systems are rooted in software, but the results of these measurements are not always dependable because they rely on the integrity of all underlying hardware components, many of which do not have a firm basis of trustworthiness. While trust in the multiple layers of a computing device can be built up through an iterative process of verifying successive levels, there must be an initial source of trust—the "root of trust"—in a system that is implicitly trustworthy.

Emerging classes of hardware components may provide the basis for dependable security measurements. These trusted hardware components generally include tamper-proof storage, which can be used to protect sensitive cryptographic keys, measurements of integral software components, and limited cryptographic functionality to perform device authentication operations. Research is needed to evaluate the utility and limitations of trusted hardware components with respect to performance of basic security measurements. In addition to establishing a solid foundation for fundamental security metrics, the research should include mechanisms for validating security measurements from the hardware to the software layer. This research would also contribute to the "composition problem," where security metrics are computed for a system composed of verifiably trusted components. See the "Composition and Compromised Systems" section below.

6.2.2.2 Trusted Identities for People, Machines, and Programs

The **National Strategy for Trusted Identities in Cyberspace (NSTIC) Program** is managing a portfolio of pilot projects that advance the theory and practice of trusted identities. Adoption of the Personal Identity Verification (PIV) card for logical access (i.e., access to IT resources) has been identified as a key metric in the *Cross Agency Goal: Cybersecurity* for 2013. Research initiatives that address impediments to deployment of PIV-based applications are critical to enhancing the security of Federal IT infrastructure. Such initiatives would also advance the NSTIC vision by demonstrating the utility of multi-factor authentication.

NSTIC's focus is on trusted identities for human users, but emerging computing environments are presenting new authentication requirements. As the "Internet of Things" begins to take shape, a need for trusted machine identities has become apparent. While there are innovative technologies on the horizon, additional research is required to determine which system properties should be assessed for monitoring.

6.2.2.3 New Technologies for Cyber Supply Chain Risk Management

Design and manufacture of computing and communications hardware and software are done globally, and the supply chains for the cyberinfrastructure that runs our Nation are now built from diverse interactions among suppliers, integrators, and servicers. Maintaining the security of the Nation's cyber infrastructure requires developing ways of validating and assuring the security of complex hardware and software systems featuring subcomponents that can come from a wide set of sources, each within different kinds of systems with differing requirements for risk tolerances. Public comments note that novel strategies are needed for improving security of integrated circuit and microprocessor design and manufacture, and that specification and verification should be expanded to include security properties. Solving cyber supply chain risk management problems requires an active policy and regulatory response working in tandem with research and development to mitigate these risks. An example of a nascent R&D effort in this area is the DARPA **Supply Chain Hardware Integrity for Electronics Defense (SHIELD) Program**, which seeks develop an advanced supply chain hardware authentication technology capability.

6.2.2.4 New Technologies for Information Sharing

Our national critical infrastructures are composed from a variety of smaller systems, the majority of which are privately owned. Information sharing among private sector operators, and among private sector owners and the government, has emerged as a key component of our long range security plans. However, effective information sharing in current legal frameworks demands controls on data that do not exist today, or are expensive to implement. Technologies to control the secondary flow of information or to anonymize data in a cost-effective manner are urgently needed to implement policy goals.

6.2.3 Within Designed-In Security

6.2.3.1 Composition and Compromised Systems

The creation of provably correct systems is a long held objective, but current methods do not scale to practical applications. Modern IT systems are highly complex, with millions of lines of code in the operating system alone. Current methods will not support the production of high-reliability systems with this level of complexity.

New software engineering methods are needed to support the production of high-reliability system specifications and of their provably correct transformation into deployable systems. There is also a need for techniques that support formal composition of high-scale and high-complexity systems to avoid emergent behaviors.

In the past, research into composition focused exclusively on systems composed of trustworthy, or at least unaltered, components. Unfortunately, alteration of one or more components in a system is all too common. An important new area of research is the composition of systems in which one or more components is assumed to be compromised. Developing systems that continue to operate correctly after being compromised is one promising opportunity to shift the cost ratio in the favor of the defender.

6.2.3.2 Architectural Resiliency
Research into fundamentally new approaches for the design of architectures underlying cyber-infrastructure is necessary so that these architectures can be made truly resilient to cyber-attack, natural disaster, and inadvertent failure. In particular, research is needed to identify and evaluate network architectures that feature a survivable core, and to develop algorithms to bootstrap widespread network restoration from this core.

6.2.4 Within Developing Scientific Foundations

6.2.4.1 Cyber Experimentation and Simulation
The role of cyber experimentation, testing, analysis, and evaluation leading to deployment of technologies is a critical element in delivering working solutions. Public comments note the importance of computational sciences and applied mathematics in understanding complex systems; comments push for the development of new tools that can be used for predictive modeling and simulation of complex systems, mathematical analysis of the behavior of complex systems, and use of models of complex systems to inform policy makers.

Our ability to conduct and learn from cyber experiments is currently underdeveloped. Similarly, in light of the growing demands to secure and defend increasingly complex cyber systems, our capabilities in cyber and cyber-physical modeling and in simulation of large-scale operations or cyber-physical systems need improvements. For instance, we need higher-fidelity capabilities to model threats and attacks in order to determine their impacts on the execution of national security missions or on the operations of critical infrastructures in the private sector.

6.2.4.2 Security Metrics
Security metrics present a target-rich opportunity for researchers. As the community shifts from a checklist-based approach to a "security culture," additional work in security metrics is required to transition from tactical metrics (e.g., compliance) to more holistic measurements, such as measuring the health of a network. Public comments emphasize the need for "metrics/benchmarks of security and trustworthiness" for hardware security as well as software security. Other opportunities for metrics target specific government and industry requirements. For example, the Administration identified improving incident reporting and response as one of the five priority areas for action. However, the associated metrics are insufficient to measure the degree of improvement. Similar opportunities exist for metrics associated with measuring the return on investment for both operational decisions and research investments.

6.3 Additional Prospective Research Areas

The framework for Federal cybersecurity R&D articulated in the 2011 Strategic Plan is not static; the framework and priorities are expected to evolve as our understanding of challenges and solutions improves. In looking forward, several broad areas of research have emerged as candidates for coordinated, multiagency efforts. While discussion of prospective research areas continues and a decision on priorities remains, examples of additional research that may strengthen the goals of the Strategic Plan are provided below.

6.3.1 Security of Cyber-Physical Systems

Our increasing reliance on cyber-physical systems, in which computing, cyberspace, and control of physical processes are interconnected, requires commensurate advances to secure them and to improve their trustworthiness. Such systems are part of the fabric of modern economies and provide critical functions in areas such as the generation and delivery of electricity, management of transportation systems, and the delivery of medical and emergency care.

Cyber-physical systems operate under constraints arising from the requirements of the physical processes being controlled. Cyber-physical systems are a significant challenge because the traditional ordering of cybersecurity priorities does not hold. Historically, computer systems are designed to meet confidentiality and integrity requirements, with availability as the distant third. For cyber-physical systems, which may be controlling the shut-off valve in a power plant or a water system, availability is often the most important requirement. There are also real-time requirements and other subtleties that differentiate these systems from the cyber world. In the energy sector, for example, stringent, millisecond operational requirements of energy delivery systems cannot be affected adversely by security technologies. Cybersecurity solutions that are developed to protect business systems and networks may not be appropriate for cyber-physical systems; additional research is needed to address requirements specific to these systems.

6.3.2 Privacy and Protected Disclosure

The January 2013 President's Council of Advisors on Science and Technology (PCAST) report on the NITRD Program[16] cited privacy and protected disclosure as a cross-cutting theme, "one that is important for every agency and mission, as huge amounts of diverse information about individuals become available in online electronic form." Multiple public comments emphasized the need for privacy research to address both how the public perceives privacy in the context of cybersecurity and how new cybersecurity technologies and practices can integrate privacy.

As highlighted in the PCAST report, a major challenge is that "no agency has primary responsibility for privacy R&D, although many agencies need a better understanding of the science of privacy and protected disclosure in an online digital world." Development of the scientific and engineering foundations of privacy R&D will require multiagency collaboration.

While some aspects of privacy are included in the scope of the Tailored Trustworthy Spaces theme, there are additional challenges that can be addressed through targeted R&D investment. The challenges, as outlined in the PCAST report, include realizing the benefits of collective personal information without compromising the privacy of individuals, achieving cybersecurity and security more broadly without unnecessary disclosure of individual information, designing systems to avoid unintended personal disclosure, empowering individuals to assert their identity and also to make

---

[16] http://www.whitehouse.gov/sites/default/files/microsites/ostp/pcast-nitrd2013.pdf

informed decisions about voluntary disclosure of information, and using the science of privacy protection to inform policy decisions.

Potential solutions to these challenges, outlined in the PCAST report and to be considered in future cybersecurity R&D Strategic Plans, include technologies such as methods to allow agents to perform analytics on large datasets while preserving privacy and confidentiality; creating and investigating formal models of privacy that combine concepts from statistics and computer science; devising methods that give individuals knowledge of what data about them is held and appropriate control over the use of that data; exploring the privacy-preserving design of human-centered systems; creating ways to educate users about, and protect users against, actions they might take that inadvertently compromise privacy; and using the outcome of research on privacy and confidentiality protection to enable privacy- and confidentiality-related policies to be application-specific.

7 Next Steps

This review amply demonstrates the value of the research framework established in the 2011 Strategic Plan. Agencies have done a commendable job implementing the Plan, as evidenced by the ongoing research initiatives highlighted in Section 5. At this early stage, there is little need for revising the four thrusts or the set of themes specified in the strategy. However, Federal agencies should consider whether to initiate new activities directed towards the topics highlighted in Section 6.

As noted in Section 6.1, the Cyber Economic Incentives theme warrants additional emphasis. The Administration's policy for protecting the Nation's critical infrastructure is predicated upon the voluntary adoption of enhanced cybersecurity technologies, as well as voluntary participation in information sharing activities. Defining economic incentives to encourage voluntary participation is a critical aspect of this policy. The February 2013 Executive Order on "Improving Critical Infrastructure Cybersecurity"[17] explicitly promotes policies to incentivize cybersecurity. Research that informs policymakers and the private sector would be invaluable.

NITRD will work to promote the security of cyber-physical systems to support other work on critical infrastructure. These activities require collaboration between the cybersecurity community and the manufacturing and process control communities. To advance this area, the NITRD Program has established the Cyber-Physical Systems (CPS) Senior Steering Group to coordinate programs, budgets, and policy recommendations for CPS research and development.

The cybersecurity R&D strategy will evolve as our understanding of threats and counter-measures improves and matures. Factors contributing to the evolution of the strategy include improved understanding of cyber risks, scientific and engineering advancements, private sector input, legislative mandates, and Administration priorities. The NITRD Program will continue to provide a forum for the refinement of the research themes through interagency coordination groups and public-private engagements.

The principal coordination groups are the NITRD CSIA IWG, with a membership of over 100 Federal program managers and directors with responsibilities for executing cybersecurity R&D programs, and the NITRD CSIA R&D SSG, consisting of senior representatives from agencies with national cybersecurity missions. NITRD also coordinates with the SCORE IWG, which focuses on R&D for national security systems. The NITRD Program and the agencies themselves also organize workshops and conferences to maintain interactions with the research community in academia and industry.

---

[17] http://www.gpo.gov/fdsys/pkg/FR-2013-02-19/pdf/2013-03915.pdf

Moving forward, the U.S. Government must continue its critical work in securing the cyber systems of today, while preparing for the threats that may emerge tomorrow. This goal is not only a formidable technical challenge, but requires fundamental shifts in the theory, design, and implementation of cyberinfrastructure to prioritize security as a critical attribute. Such a shift can only be addressed by a continuous, proactive, and comprehensive national cybersecurity R&D enterprise consisting of a healthy ecosystem of coordinated academic, Federal, and industry research. The Administration is dedicated to achieving the goal of creating a "Trustworthy Cyberspace" that both enables Federal agencies to meet their mission goals and allows all Americans to communicate, interact, and thrive in the modern digital world.

8 Appendix: Acronyms

AFOSR	Air Force Office of Scientific Research
AFRL	Air Force Research Laboratory
APP	Automatic Privacy Protection Program
ARCSYNE	Active Repositioning in Cyberspace for Synchronized Evasion Program
ARL	Army Research Laboratory
ARO	Army Research Office
ASCR	Advanced Scientific Computing Research Program
ASD (R&E)	Assistant Secretary of Defense for Research and Engineering
BAA	Broad Agency Announcement
C3I	Command, Control, Communications, and Information Systems
C4ISR	Command, Control, Communications, Computers, Intelligence, Surveillance, Reconnaissance
CEDS	Cybersecurity for Energy Delivery Systems Program
CFT	Cyber Fast Track Program
CMC	Cyber Measurement Campaign
CPS	Cyber-Physical System
CRA	Cyber Security Collaborative Research Alliance
CRASH	Clean-Slate Design of Resilient, Adaptive, Secure Hosts Program
CSIA	Cyber Security and Information Assurance
CTP	Cyber Transition to Practice
DARPA	Defense Advanced Research Projects Agency
DHS	Department of Homeland Security
DoD	Department of Defense
DoD Cyber COI	DoD Cyber S&T Community of Interest
DOE	Department of Energy
FFRDC	Federally Funded Research and Development Center
HACMS	High-Assurance Cyber Military Systems Program
HIPAA	Health Insurance Portability and Accountability Act
IARPA	Intelligence Advanced Research Projects Activity
IETF	Internet Engineering Task Force
IP	Internet Protocol
ITA	International Technology Alliance
IWG	Interagency Working Group
JSCoRE	Journal of Sensitive Cybersecurity Research and Engineering
Mobius	Model-Based Evaluation of System Dependability and Security Program
MRC	Mission-oriented Resilient Clouds Program

MURI	Multidisciplinary University Research Initiative
NCCoE	National Cybersecurity Center of Excellence
NCO	National Coordination Office
NITRD	Networking and Information Technology Research and Development
NIST	National Institute of Standards and Technology
NSA	National Security Agency
NSF	National Science Foundation
NSTC	National Science and Technology Council
NSTIC	National Strategy for Trusted Identities in Cyberspace
ODNI	Office of the Director of National Intelligence
ONC	Office of the National Coordinator for Health Information Technology
ONR	Office of Naval Research
OSD	Office of the Secretary of Defense
OSTP	Office of Science and Technology Policy
PCAST	President's Council of Advisors on Science and Technology
PI	Principal Investigator
R&D	Research and Development
S&T	Science and Technology
SaTC	Secure and Trustworthy Cyberspace Program
SBIR	Small Business Innovation Research
SCAP	Security Content Automation Protocol
SCI	Secure Coding Initiative
SCORE	Special Cyber Operations Research and Engineering
SEI	Software Engineering Institute
SFS	CyberCorps®: Scholarship for Service Program
SGCC	Smart Grid Interoperability Panel Cybersecurity Committee
SGIP-CSWG	Smart Grid Interoperability Panel-Cyber Security Working Group
SHARPS	Strategic Healthcare IT Advanced Research Projects on Security Program
SHIELD	Supply Chain Hardware Integrity for Electronics Defense Program
SPAR	Security and Privacy Assurance Research Program
SSG	Senior Steering Group
STONESOUP	Securely Taking On New Executable Software of Uncertain Provenance Program
TCIPG	Trustworthy Cyber Infrastructure for the Power Grid Program
THaW	Trustworthy Health and Wellness Project
TTCP	The Technical Cooperation Program
TTP	Transition To Practice Program
UARC	University Affiliated Research Center